T0040929

JOHN HARBISON

SIMPLE DAYLIGHT

Soprano and Piano

AMP-8086

First printing: October 1995

Associated Music Publishers, Inc.

DISTRIBUTED BY

7777 W. BLUEMOUND RD. P.O. BOX 13819 MILWAUKEE, WI 53213

Program Note

It has been a source of satisfaction to me that the first performers and listeners of *Simple Daylight* have been especially struck by the poems, and by the strong musical responses elicited by the poems. I have been grateful for Michael Fried's work in many ways, most obviously in my previous settings of his texts in *Three Harp Songs* (1972) and *The Flower-Fed Buffaloes* (1976).

My ordering of his poems makes a sequence closer in tone to a Bach Cantata text than to a nineteenth-century song cycle, and evokes a kind of sub-cutaneous narrative very favorable for musical purposes, but no doubt unintended by the poet.

Simple Daylight was commissioned by Lincoln Center. The dedication to its first singer, Dawn Upshaw, represents my complete confidence in sending her into uncharted waters, as well as my intuition that she would enjoy the complete, motet-like partnership with the pianist that the cycle requires.

—JOHN HARBISON

Simple Daylight *was premiered on May 22, 1990 at the Herbst Theatre in San Francisco with Dawn Upshaw, soprano and Alan Feinberg, piano.*

duration: ca. 16 minutes

recording: Elektra Nonesuch CD79189-2/4,
Dawn Upshaw Soprano, Gilbert Kalish, piano

Japan

Tired and empty,
I occupy a winterized log cabin
In a clearing in a snowy wood
In a country that might be Japan.

Each morning I catechize myself
In the hope that there has been a change
Either from or into the new man
It appears I've partly become.

Lunch arrives in a wicker basket
That later will be taken away.
But when I rush to the window
The encircling snow lies undefiled.

Toward midnight I shall step outside
And expose my face to the stars
And weep for all the hurt I've caused.
May their beauty appease me.

My best moments are those
When, in default of inspiration,
My hand rests lightly on the wrist
Of the one who writes.

Simple Daylight

It's true—if there were life after death
In an underworld it would be simple daylight
I would miss most, would grieve for
Inconsolably, would braid into every poem,
Every lament, such as this one,
For what was lost.

Somewhere a Seed

Somewhere a seed falls to the ground
That will become a tree
That will someday be felled
From which thin shafts will be extracted
To be made into arrows
To be fitted with warheads
One of which, some day when you least expect it,
While a winter sun is shining
On a river of ice
And you feel furthest from self-pity,
Will pierce your shit-filled heart.

Your Name

That passionate monosyllable, your name,
Like some wounded animal's all but inarticulate
Cry, when the familiar hurt returns, on dragging legs,
After an interlude of sleep or natural anesthesia,
Spoken over and over my own lips, wakes me.

The Wild Irises

Dying of thirst,
I long to share the fate of the wild irises
Each raindrop must seem to whom the size of a boulder
Flung down to devastate them with what they need.

Odor

Your perfume, or odor–
Waking I remember it, my body
Remembers it, my body when dead will remember it
In its bones, and when after incineration
The bones themselves are pulverized and dispersed upon
   the air
As tiny motes of ash, they too will remember
(Dancing in the sunlight, jostled by larger molecules)
Your odor without a name.

—MICHAEL FRIED

These poems appear in Michael Fried's *To the Center of the Earth,* Farrar, Straus and Giroux, New York 1994 and are used by permission. Certain alterations of detail, at variance with the published versions, were introduced by the composer for dramatic purposes, with the sanction of the poet.

to Dawn Upshaw

SIMPLE DAYLIGHT
I. Japan

Michael Fried

John Harbison

* Use of the pedal is by no means confined to the passages indicated.

Copyright © 1990 by Associated Music Publishers Inc. (BMI), New York, NY
All Rights Reserved International Copyright Secured Printed in U.S.A.
Warning: Unauthorized reproduction of this publication is
prohibited by Federal Law and subject to criminal prosecution.

-ing in a snow-y wood In a coun-try that might be

Ja-pan.

Each

morn-ing I cat-e-chize my-self

-ket That lat-er will be tak-en a-way.

But when I rush to the win - dow

The en-cir - - cling snow lies ___ un - de-

filed.

II. Simple Daylight

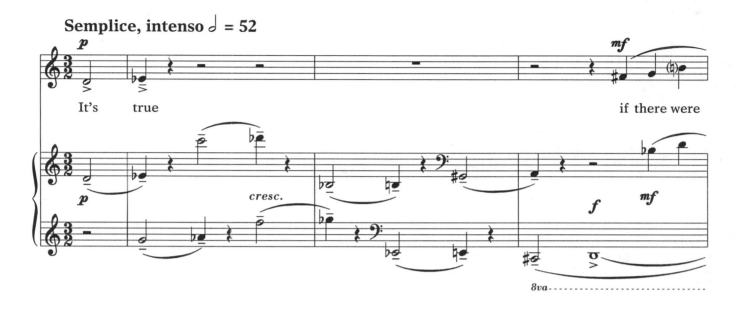

Semplice, intenso ♩ = 52

It's true ... if there were

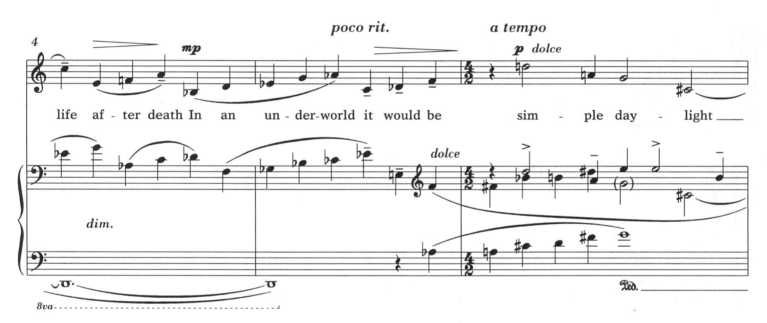

life af-ter death In an un-der-world it would be sim - ple day - light____

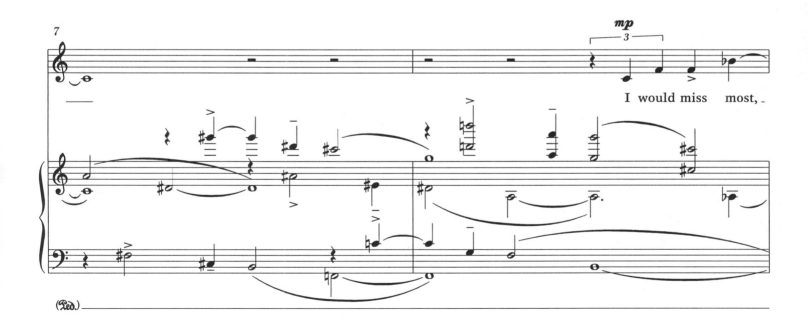

I would miss most,____

III. Somewhere a Seed

IV. Your Name

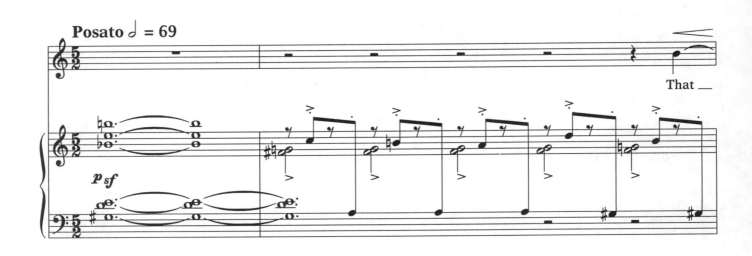

V. The Wild Irises

VI. Odor